My Survival

A Girl on Schindler's List

OTHER TITLES YOU MIGHT BE INTERESTED IN:

Signs of Survival: A Memoir of the Holocaust
by Renee Hartman and Joshua M. Greene

Hidden Like Anne Frank: 14 True Stories of Survival
by Marcel Prins and Peter Henk Steenhuis

Survivors: True Stories of Children in the Holocaust
by Allan Zullo and Mara Bovsun

Prisoner B-3087
by Alan Gratz, a novel based on the true story
by Ruth and Jack Gruener

My Survival

A GIRL ON SCHINDLER'S LIST

A memoir by

Rena Finder with Joshua M. Greene

Scholastic Inc.

Copyright © 2019 by Rena Finder and Joshua M. Greene

This book was originally published in hardcover by Scholastic Press in 2019.

All rights reserved. Published by Scholastic Inc., *Publishers since 1920*. SCHOLASTIC and associated logos are trademarks and/or registered trademarks of Scholastic Inc.

The publisher does not have any control over and does not assume any responsibility for author or third-party websites or their content.

No part of this publication may be reproduced, stored in a retrieval system, or transmitted in any form or by any means, electronic, mechanical, photocopying, recording, or otherwise, without written permission of the publisher. For information regarding permission, write to Scholastic Inc., Attention: Permissions Department, 557 Broadway, New York, NY 10012.

ISBN 978-1-338-59382-2

2 2024

Printed in the U.S.A.   23

This edition first printing 2022

Book design by Maeve Norton

With love and gratitude
to Margot Stern Strom,
cofounder of Facing History and Ourselves,
who gave survivors a place to share their stories

1.

October 1944—

AUSCHWITZ DEATH CAMP

IT WAS BITTER COLD the night German police forced me and my mother into a cattle car and sent us from Plaszow, Poland, to Auschwitz, the largest of all Nazi killing centers. The train was made up of two cattle cars. There were 150 women prisoners crammed into each of the two cars. I was fourteen years old, one of the youngest. We arrived at Auschwitz late at night. Guards slammed open the doors of the cattle car and yelled at us to jump out. Then they marched us into a long wooden barrack with rows of benches along the walls.

"Take off all your clothes!" the guards shouted. "You will be brought back here to collect your things later—after your shower."

The guards shoved us into a room maybe twenty feet by twenty feet. It was dark, but we could see pipes running the length of the ceiling. Back home in Krakow, we had heard scary rumors about what happened to Jews in concentration camps. What kind of shower was this? Were we going to die?

If you were not there in the death camp at Auschwitz, you cannot imagine it, and I cannot truly describe it. Still, for most of my adult life, I have been trying as best I can to teach about the Holocaust in middle-grade schools and colleges, in church groups and synagogues. Like many other survivors, I feel an obligation to tell my story again and again. The Holocaust was the scientifically designed, state-sponsored murder of the Jewish people by Nazi Germany and its allies. The Holocaust should never be forgotten and should never happen again—but how can we protect against that? You, dear reader, can help. One person with courage to stand up for the innocent can make a big difference.

I should know. I'm alive thanks to someone who refused to stand by and do nothing. His name was Oskar Schindler.

2.

1930s–

ANOTHER WORLD

TO UNDERSTAND THE STORY you are about to read, it will help to know something about my childhood and where I came from. Please keep in mind that today I am ninety years old. These are the memories of a girl in her early teens, and some memories change over time. I cannot promise you that everything happened exactly as I am recalling. After so many years, some details may be less than perfect.

What I can promise you is that everything I tell you is truthful and that these things did happen.

I was born in 1929 in Krakow, Poland's historic capital city. Krakow was a center of the nation's artistic and cultural life. It had a famous university attended by students from around the world. Electric streetcars crisscrossed the city, bringing people to offices, museums, and libraries.

I lived with my mother, Rosa, and my father, Moses, in one of Krakow's many apartment buildings. Our building was a few blocks from the center of the city and next door to a Franciscan monastery. There was a balcony off the stairway landing below our fourth-floor apartment. From the balcony, I could look into the monastery's backyard, where there were fruit trees and flowering bushes. In the early morning hours, monks walked slowly around the backyard in their long brown robes, praying on strands of wooden beads. My memories of early childhood are, for the most part, like that orchard: calm and pleasant.

My parents' bedroom had a large wooden clothes closet. In the kitchen was an iron cookstove that burned coal. A Polish woman came once a week to clean, and on cold days she took a metal bucket, walked down four flights of marble stairs to the cellar, filled the bucket with coal, and carried it back upstairs. Heat from three coal-burning ovens warmed the whole apartment.

I remember other details from my childhood. Our main language at home was Polish, but my mother hired a tutor who taught me German. Because of all the later horrors that happened to me and my family at the hands of Nazi Germany, once I came to America, I never wanted to hear German spoken ever again.

My father was a good man: loving, attentive to me and my mother, and always looking to do good for others. He earned a living as a salesman for a company that made surgical instruments and hospital supplies. He left Krakow every Monday morning by train to visit out-of-town customers and returned on Friday in time for the start of the Sabbath. The Sabbath—the time between sunset on Friday and sunset on Saturday—has always been the most sacred part of the week for Jews. During those twenty-four hours, religious Jews dedicate their time to religious study and do no work. Even turning on a light switch is considered work and forbidden on the Sabbath.

I was an only child, but my mother had six siblings and my father had seven. My mother's parents, Hannah and Isaac, had their own apartment around the corner from us. I had cousins who lived on the other side of the Vistula River, which flowed around the city, and my mother's siblings lived in Berlin, Germany, about eight hours away by train. So as a child, I was surrounded by family. In summer, we all came together and rented a cottage in the village called Zawoja, near a famous mountain known as

Baba Gura ("Baba Mountain"), where we hiked, swam in freshwater streams, and picked juicy strawberries and wild mushrooms.

There was an elderly woman who took care of us on summer days while my parents, aunts, and uncles went hiking up Baba Mountain. One time, when the grown-ups were out mountain climbing, the sky grew dark, a heavy rainstorm began, and thunder shook the windows. We kids weren't so scared, but the nanny was terrified and insisted we all kneel down and pray. It felt funny—what did a bunch of Jewish kids know about Christian prayers?—but we did it anyway to make her happy.

These days, when I'm invited to speak about my childhood, students often ask if I experienced anti-Semitism. Yes, I did. Many of our neighbors didn't bother hiding their hatred of Jews. Of course, each person who endured the Holocaust has particular memories, and conditions were different depending on where people grew up and how they were treated. In my case, growing up in Krakow, the anti-Semitism was obvious. You could see it in people's faces when they looked at you. Sometimes they did worse than just look, as I found out when I was six years old and starting school.

Krakow had a large Jewish population: about 60,000 of the city's 200,000 residents were Jews. There was a private Jewish girls' school, but it was a few miles away from our building, and my parents didn't like the idea of me walking such a long distance alone. Instead, they sent me to a public school around the corner from our house. The school was so close that my mother could stand on the balcony of our apartment and watch me playing in the schoolyard, to be sure I was safe.

My first day in kindergarten, a few of us five- and

six-year-olds were playing hopscotch in the school-yard. Without warning, one of the girls picked up a stone and threw it at me.

"Go home, you dirty Jew!" she yelled.

Did I hear her right? I was too shocked to say anything. That afternoon when school ended, I ran home and told my mother what had happened. "Why did that girl call me *dirty*?" I asked. "I'm not dirty. I took a shower just this morning."

My mother told me some people called us dirty just because our religion was different from theirs, and they didn't like us. That made no sense to me, but as a six-year-old, what did I understand of the world? I loved everybody and was happy playing with the other girls in my school. Who cared which religion they belonged to?

The next day, my mother took me by the hand and we walked to the local library, where she looked for a book that might explain anti-Semitism. I don't remember if she found such a book, but I do remember her telling me, "In life, not everybody is going to like you, and you're not going to like everyone, either. But that's no reason to hate them."

My mother and father were friendly with the Polish woman who was superintendent of our building. She had three sons. My parents helped her sons find jobs, and out of appreciation she invited us to join them for their Christmas holiday dinner. Still, that kind of friendship between Jews and non-Jews was rare.

Our family went back many generations in Poland, and my parents were strongly patriotic. We loved our country. My mother's oldest brother, Zigmund, had been a surgeon for the Polish army during the First World War. When he was killed on the battlefield, the army awarded him one of its most prestigious medals. I used to take Uncle Zigmund's medal to school for show-and-tell. But having an uncle who was a war hero didn't matter to kids whose parents had taught them to hate Jews, and the Jewish students always had to be on the lookout for stone throwers.

Sometime in the spring of 1938, when I was nine years old, my aunt Helen and my uncle Benjamin and their two children, Rita and Jenny, visited us from Berlin. In the evening, the grown-ups waited until they thought the children were asleep and then whispered about Adolf Hitler, Germany's dictator, and the terrible things his Nazi Party was doing to Jews. My aunt and uncle said they were afraid the Nazis would force them to give up their tailoring business and send them to a concentration camp.

I had no idea what that meant. What was a concentration camp? Could any of this be true? It was so frightening, I didn't sleep that night.

3.

1939–

WAR

ON SEPTEMBER 1, 1939, the German army invaded Poland. My family was on vacation near Baba Mountain at the time, and we heard the news on our radio. My father was away on a business trip. He also heard the news on a radio and left his trip early to join us at our summer cottage. "We must return to Krakow immediately," he told us. We threw our clothes into suitcases and made our way to the train station, where there were hundreds of people rushing to get home. My family and I managed to squeeze into a crowded compartment, and the train departed for Krakow.

A few hours later, we arrived at the Krakow station. The sky was filled with the sounds of air-raid sirens and German fighter planes buzzing over the city. We hurried home and ran downstairs with other tenants to the air-raid shelter in the cellar. Through the cellar walls we heard bombs exploding in the distance. The German army was approaching. The bombing finally stopped, and we mounted the stairs to our apartment, terrified about what might happen next.

The German army occupied Krakow in the first week of September 1939. They marched through the city in parade fashion, their boots pounding on the pavement, while tanks rolled down the streets and shook the ground like an earthquake.

Hitler hated Jews. We had known that for some

time already. But now his Nazi troops occupied our city, and my father and his brothers gathered in our apartment to discuss what to do. Surely, they agreed, the Germans wouldn't harm women and children. It was the men who were in danger and should run away.

"Don't worry," they told us. "The German invasion won't last long, and soon we will all be together again."

My father and his brothers stuffed food and clothes into backpacks, kissed us goodbye, joined other men from our neighborhood on the street, and together they all walked out of the city. I did not know if I would ever see my father again.

Weeks went by with no word of whether my father was alive or not. Finally, two months after he left Krakow, I was standing outside our apartment building when one of the men from our street came walking home. If this neighbor is back, I told myself, then maybe my father will also come home soon.

The next day, he did. My mother and I hugged and kissed him as though he had returned from the grave.

The only way we could remain in Krakow and not get deported or killed was if my father succeeded in getting a work permit. We knew we might be killed, because the Nazis posted big placards on the streets and newspaper kiosks, warning Jews of the consequences of staying without a permit. A permit was a government card that certified the bearer worked at a job the Germans needed done, such as construction or business. My father had most recently worked for a pharmaceutical company, going to drugstores to sell goods. But these and other jobs were taken away from Jews, and he became unemployed.

One of our apartment superintendent's sons had become head of the supply company where my father used to work. With this man's help, my father was able to resume his job selling hospital supplies, which qualified him for a work permit. At least for the moment, we were legally allowed to stay in Krakow.

But that didn't mean we were safe. Life for Jews during the Nazi occupation of Poland grew more dangerous every day. For example, one day my father bought me a puppy. My mother wasn't so happy about that. She said, "If that puppy makes a mess on my floor, you will have to give it away." I had no idea how to train a puppy. Every evening I took the puppy out for a walk so he wouldn't dirty the floor. By then the Germans had imposed a curfew, meaning Jews were not allowed to be out on the street past a certain hour. One evening, I took the puppy for a walk later than usual, and two German officers walked by and stopped me.

"What are you doing out so late?" one of the officers said.

I was so scared I could hardly speak. I pointed to my dog.

"Go home!" the officer yelled. "And don't be out late again!"

It was so frightening. My parents saw it all from a window of our building. The next day, they gave the puppy away to the woman who delivered milk to our building. I didn't object. It was a choice between losing my pet or possibly my life.

By late 1939, when I was ten years old, life for Jews in Krakow began growing even worse. It seemed like every day a new law was passed against us. One day, the Germans announced that we could no longer own radios or bicycles. Then they announced that Jews could no longer attend religious services. If we were caught practicing our religion, it would mean immediate deportation or death.

After that, we secretly held religious services in our apartment. Sometimes, when the adults were upstairs praying, children downstairs in the street watched to make sure no Germans were coming. If a German officer walked by, the kids on the street signaled to other kids at the second-floor window. Those kids ran to tell the adults, and everyone hid their prayer books and prayer shawls.

Then Jews were ordered to wear white armbands with a blue Star of David stitched on it. The Star of David was a symbol of the Jewish people, and because Nazis did not accept Jews as real human beings, the armband was their way of telling everyone "this person is less than human."

In December 1939, the German authorities announced that Jewish children could no longer attend school. My classmates and I were still young, and our parents wanted us to continue learning, so they contacted teachers and paid them to give private lessons to me and my Jewish girlfriends. To avoid drawing attention to these illegal classes, we met in a different home each day and hid our books and papers so no one would know what we were doing.

Next, Jews were no longer allowed to use public transportation. We were forbidden from even walking on the sidewalk and had to walk in the gutter. There was worse to come. The German police threw Jews out of their own shops and gave their businesses to Polish non-Jews. Then they froze our families' bank accounts. With no source of income and no access to our own savings, we had to be careful with whatever cash we had left.

Another new law forbade Polish people from doing any business with Jews. This meant that even Jews who had some cash could not buy food in grocery stores. We lived around the corner from a bakery, and at three o'clock in the morning, I would stand in line, hoping the baker would agree to sell me a little bread. The only place we still could buy food was the black market, which meant from people who sold food illegally. If caught, we and they would be arrested and beaten, or worse.

Across Europe, German armies were conquering one country after another, and rumors filtered back to Krakow that Jews in those countries were being murdered by the tens of thousands. We told ourselves that surely the rest of the world must know what was happening. Surely, England would come to our rescue, or perhaps France or America.

But where were they? Where was the rest of the world? How much longer would we have to suffer? Could it possibly get any worse?

4.

1940-41-

THE KRAKOW GHETTO

BY THE SPRING OF 1940, the Jewish citizens of Krakow were forced to do hard labor every day. This included older people, who were made to clean the streets. No Jew was safe. Several times, I saw Germans grab people off the street and send them away. The police looked in particular for men who wore beards and sidelocks, which are long, curly sideburns. Religious men grew a beard and sidelocks as a sign of their deep faith in God. The German soldiers grabbed them, cut off their hair, and then drove them away in trucks. The grown-ups never told us where the police took these men. They didn't want to shock us with the truth.

One morning, my parents and I had to renew our permits to remain in Krakow. Children under twelve were not allowed to stay, and I was barely eleven. Fortunately, I was tall for my age, and my father altered my birth certificate to say I was twelve. We presented ourselves at the government offices and stood in a line with about two thousand other people waiting to get permits. Hundreds of German soldiers walked up and down the line, armed with rifles and revolvers. Many of the soldiers held huge dogs on leashes. I had never in my life seen dogs so big.

Just as the agent was about to hand us our permit renewals, trucks arrived. Soldiers jumped down and walked over to the people waiting for their permits. The soldiers separated out the Jewish men and shoved them into the trucks. Husbands and fathers were dragged away from their families, and people were crying and screaming. The Germans fired guns in the air to quiet the crowd, and their fierce dogs barked. We were terrified.

Less than five hundred feet away from this chaos and screaming, on one of the main streets of the city, Polish people went about their business as though nothing were happening, as though we Jews didn't exist. Outside the area of the roundup, people pretended to not hear or see anything. How was this possible? I asked myself. Are we not all Polish citizens? My father and his brothers had fought for Poland in World War I. Yet here were our neighbors, the people my family had fought for, turning their backs on us.

Just before the soldiers could take my father away, the permit officer stamped our papers and handed them over. "You can stay in Krakow," he told my father. "But you must leave your apartment and move your family into the ghetto."

———◆◆◆———

The ghetto was a series of streets that contained 320 apartment buildings. Before becoming a ghetto, these buildings housed about three thousand people. The Germans moved those residents elsewhere and crammed more than sixteen thousand Jews into the same crowded space. Flyers hung on every street corner of the city, announcing that all Jews were to relocate to the ghetto no later than March 20, 1941.

My father brought a pushcart to our apartment building. We loaded it with pots, pans, towels, blankets, and the wooden bed from my parents' room. We handed our apartment keys to the super and walked away from our beautiful home. It was a short walk from our building to the ghetto, maybe only twenty minutes, but this was in March and the weather was still frigid. Before leaving, we dressed in as many layers of clothing as possible. I wore three pairs of pants and four sweaters and felt like a teddy bear.

From the street, I looked back at our building and cried over having to leave behind my copies of *Anne of Green Gables, Oliver Twist, David Copperfield,* and other favorite books. I also had a collection of Shirley Temple dolls that I loved, and they stayed behind as well. We walked through the streets of Krakow, pulling the wagon that contained everything we had left in the world. From the sidewalks, Polish people spit, threw stones at us, and yelled, "Good riddance! Go, Jews! Don't ever come back!" We never did anything to them, and as an innocent eleven-year-old, I couldn't understand why they hated us so much.

———◆◆◆———

We approached the ghetto with hundreds of other Jews holding suitcases, blankets, and whatever else they were able to carry. The Germans had built a brick wall around the ghetto nearly ten feet high. German soldiers and Polish police patrolled everywhere. We walked through the gates, and it felt as if my life had ended.

Inside the ghetto my father led us to the place where one of his brothers lived. It was an old four-story stone building. People with grim expressions were moving in and out of the building. My uncle let us into his apartment and gave us a half-hearted smile. No one had any illusions about our predicament. This was not a happy family reunion.

The apartment was tiny: just two little rooms and a teeny kitchen with a small sink. A few weeks before the war started, my parents had taken me to see the animated movie *Snow White and the Seven Dwarfs*. When I saw that miniature sink, I said to my mother, "This is good for the dwarfs, but how will it work for all of us?"

My uncle and his wife and child lived in one room;

my mother and father and I lived in the second room—which we found out we had to share with yet another family, named Goldberg. There were three Goldbergs: the wife, the husband, and the husband's sister. My parents screwed hooks into the middle walls of the room, stretched a rope from one hook to the other, threw a blanket over the rope, and that's how six people shared one small room.

"Don't worry," my father said, not sounding convinced. "Someone will find out what's happening and come to save us." No one ever did.

The Germans had taken over all the Jewish-owned businesses in Krakow and relocated some of them inside the ghetto. Tailors, dressmakers, shoemakers, and others who used to have their own shops were now slave laborers for Nazis, who paid them nothing and forced them to work long days and nights.

My mother and I were assigned to a printing shop.

Trucks arrived each week from outside the ghetto, and workers unloaded rolls of paper as tall as me. We were responsible for positioning the rolls onto a big machine that folded the paper and turned out notebooks. We stacked the notebooks into piles and wrapped the piles in bundles with string. The bundles of notebooks were then trucked out of the ghetto and sold to paper shops in Nazi-occupied cities across Europe. We worked in that printing shop twelve hours a day, seven days a week.

One of my mother's sisters and her husband had also been forced to move into the ghetto. Their youngest daughter was a beautiful five-year-old named Jenny, who became like a younger sister to me. She had blond hair, blue eyes, and the sweetness of an angel. I did not know it then, but later I learned that it was rare for a child as young as Jenny to be in the ghetto, because parents with small children were denied work permits and deported to concentration camps to be killed. If Jenny was to survive, her parents understood there was no choice but to hide her in our apartment.

The day my aunt and uncle and Jenny's older sister were deported, they said goodbye to Jenny, and from that moment on, my little cousin was our responsibility. Each morning, all the people in our apartment left for their various jobs in the ghetto while Jenny stayed in the apartment alone. She understood that she had to be quiet, but what would a five-year-old do for twelve hours waiting for us to come home? I had no idea, and all day long while stacking notebooks in the printing shop, I worried about her and hoped she would still be there when we returned.

In the ghetto, I met a girl who would become my best friend for life. Her name was Sonia. She was six months older than me and attended underground classes with me and two other girls. Sonia and I quickly became friends. Sonia had an older sister named Blanca. Sometimes, when Blanca wasn't looking, Sonia showed me how Blanca put on makeup, which was frowned upon at our age. That was the kind of funny, adventurous person Sonia was, always taking risks and looking for a bit of sunshine. But even Sonia could not find sunshine on the day her mother was sent to the concentration camp Auschwitz.

Auschwitz was one of thousands of camps built by the Nazis between 1933 and 1945. These camps included concentration camps, labor camps, prisoner-of-war camps, transit camps, and killing centers, which were called extermination camps or death camps. By 1942, the purpose of the Nazi Party was to kill every Jew in Europe, and in May the German authorities began deporting Jews by train— we called them transports—from the Krakow ghetto to camps across Europe.

In some camps, prisoners were worked to death. In

other camps, prisoners were suffocated in gas chambers and their bodies burned to ashes in crematoria ovens. The Nazis called this mass murder of Jews the Final Solution. Auschwitz was the largest of all Nazi killing centers.

At night in the ghetto, in our tiny apartment, my mother, my father, Jenny, and I ate a meal of watery soup and a little bread. We never knew if soldiers were going to show up that night and send us to one of the camps. When Sonia and I had to go from one place in the ghetto to another, we never knew if soldiers were going to walk by and shoot us. So wherever we went, we ran. Every moment in the Krakow ghetto was dangerous. Any second, you could be killed. When you left your home, you didn't know if you would come back.

You just never knew.

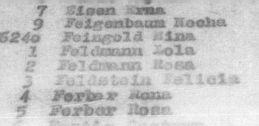

5.

1942–

Liquidation of the Krakow Ghetto

WE SAW DEATH EVERY day in the Krakow ghetto. My father had a good friend named Rudy. They used to play cards together. One day my father came home with an ashen face. He told us that he and Rudy had been standing in front of the ghetto hospital when a German officer walked by, fired his gun, and killed Rudy. The German had no reason to

33

shoot Rudy, other than because he was a Jew.

On December 31, 1942, German soldiers burst into our apartment and arrested my father. It no longer mattered that my father had a work permit. It no longer mattered that he was a good person who never did anything wrong. The Germans decided the time had come for him to die. Imagine being thirteen years old and seeing your father marched away to be murdered.

Later, I found out the reason my father had been arrested. There was another Jew in the ghetto who was jealous of my father's popularity and had lied to the police that my father was active in the underground. The underground was a secret organization of young men and women who fought the Germans by stealing their weapons, blowing up Nazi offices, and enlisting others to resist the German occupation of Poland. In the Krakow ghetto, there was such an underground group of young resisters, but my father never had anything to do with them.

My mother and I were frantic and looked for someone who could get my father released, but we had no luck. The Germans kept him in the ghetto jail for one week, then put him on a transport to Auschwitz. In my eyes, my father was the smartest and strongest man in the world, and I was sure nothing would happen to him. Somehow, I told myself, he would figure out how to survive. Those were the hopes of a naïve thirteen-year-old. What did I know about Auschwitz or the horrors that happened there? The day the Germans deported my father was the day I saw him for the last time.

In the beginning, before the Germans decided to liquidate—meaning shut down—the Krakow ghetto, few people knew where the transports were going. The Germans lied that the trains took Jews to farms where they grew food for the German army, and many Jews in the ghetto forced themselves to believe this was true. After all, who wanted to think their family members were being sent away to be killed?

But then the German government started sending made-up postcards to people in the ghetto that read, "Sorry to inform you that this or that person from your family has died of natural causes." For a while, the Germans even sent boxes of ashes with a note: "Here are the remains of your loved one." Then we heard that the Krakow ghetto was to be liquidated, and even the most hopeful Jews understood the truth: No one was being sent away to work on a farm. They were being sent away to die.

The only Jews allowed to live were those whom the Germans deemed "fit for work," meaning between the ages of twelve and fifty-five. My mother's parents were nearly seventy years old. To save them from the transports, my mother and her younger sister brought their parents out into the courtyard of our building and told them to hide under a pile of leaves. My grandparents told me to hide with them. I wasn't sure why, because I was thirteen and allowed to stay in the ghetto, but I did what they asked me to do. My grandparents and I stretched out on our stomachs and crawled under a pile of leaves and dirt.

"Stay still and quiet," my mother whispered to us, then she and my aunt left to go to their work.

From under the pile of dirt, I felt the ground shake as trucks carrying soldiers rolled through the ghetto. A few minutes later I heard soldiers marching into our building and going door to door, rounding up any old people they found hiding. Just to make their elderly Jewish prisoners more miserable, the soldiers took chairs and tables from their apartments and threw them out the window. Furniture crashed on the courtyard ground. Then the soldiers marched their prisoners down the stairs, out through the gates of the courtyard, and lined them up against a brick wall. We heard shots and people screaming. After a while, it became quiet.

Some hours later, my mother returned from work.

"You can come out now," she said. "Everybody is gone." My grandparents and I stood up and brushed the leaves off our clothes. Just when we thought my grandparents were safe, something terrible happened. Two German soldiers making a final inspection of the ghetto walked into the courtyard. Seeing the dirt and leaves in my grandparents' hair, it was obvious they had been hiding. My grandmother bent down and whispered to me, "We'll be okay." She took my grandfather's hand, and the soldiers marched them away. I will never forget the expression on my mother's face, watching her parents walking away to be murdered. It was horrible.

We went back to our apartment and did our best to repair the damage done by the soldiers, but some destruction can't be repaired.

———◆◆◆———

The liquidation of the Krakow ghetto continued. For four days, German soldiers went door to door rounding up Jews. In those four days, two thousand men, women, and children were sent to the Plaszow concentration camp two miles away; three thousand were sent to be murdered in Auschwitz; and two thousand more were killed on the spot. The Germans gathered together all the other Jews—those who possessed work permits—and told them they would be relocated to Plaszow. Many of the ghetto workshops had already been relocated there, including the printing shop where my mother and I had been assigned.

We assembled by the gates of the ghetto and set out on the forced march to Plaszow concentration camp.

6.

THE PLASZOW
CONCENTRATION CAMP

CHILDREN UNDER THE AGE of ten were not allowed into the Plaszow camp. Instead, before Jewish parents left on the march to Plaszow, police forced them to send their young children to the Krakow ghetto's orphanage. Some parents tried to bring their little children with them to Plaszow by giving them a sleeping pill and hiding them in backpacks. My cousin Jenny was too big to hide in a backpack, but I was desperate to bring her with us to Plaszow. Even though the concentration camp would be terrible, at least if we were together, I could look after her. An idea came to me: I would hide her under my long coat.

As my mother and I approached the gates of the ghetto, a policeman saw Jenny's feet under my coat. He opened the coat and looked at my beautiful little cousin, who was clearly less than ten years old.

"You can't take her," he said. "She's too young. She must stay here. Let the orphanage take care of her."

My mother and I knew some of the people who ran the orphanage and told ourselves Jenny would be fine staying with them. What choice did we have? I took Jenny by the hand and together we walked back inside the ghetto. It was only a few blocks, down empty streets, past empty buildings. We arrived at the orphanage. Several hundred children had been assembled outside the building. I recognized the woman supervising them. She was a friend of my mother.

"Don't worry," she told me, taking Jenny by the hand. "I will take care of her."

I kissed Jenny goodbye and walked back to join my mother by the gates of the ghetto for the two-mile march to Plaszow.

Police started the march, and just as we began walking away from the ghetto, we heard gunshots. I felt a terrible chill. Surely the shots were coming from someplace else, not from the orphanage. But as we continued toward Plaszow, someone came up and whispered that the children in the orphanage were being murdered.

Could it be true? My mother and I walked on, speechless, too shaken to say anything. Dogs barked and the Nazi security police, known as the SS, yelled, *"Mach schnell!* Hurry!" We quickened our pace and marched to Plaszow, still hearing shots being fired inside the ghetto.

We arrived at the Plaszow camp, which was a total size of about a hundred city blocks. There were eighty-eight barracks in the camp, housing about twenty-five thousand inmates, all of them Jews. When we arrived, police divided Jews from the Krakow ghetto into groups and marched them to their assigned barracks. My mother and I were pushed into a crowded barrack with bunk beds three tiers high, like wooden shelves too narrow to sit up in. Apart from the barracks, Plaszow had one filthy latrine that was always overflowing, a "clinic" that never had any medical supplies, and workshops where prisoners labored each day.

We adjusted to the daily routine. At four o'clock in the morning, guards made a young musician from Krakow play his bugle to wake us. Prisoners ran outside and stood at attention for hours while roll call was taken. This was in winter, and many mornings were freezing cold. German officers went up and down the lines of prisoners. If one person was missing, the roll call had to be taken again, and we were forced to stand for more hours, often in rain or snow. There were sick people among the prisoners who could not stand for long. But if they sat down, it meant they were not strong enough to work, and guards dragged them off to be killed.

We were always hungry in the Plaszow camp. *Hungry* as most people understand that word today is different from hungry in a concentration camp. *Hungry* in a camp meant a twisting, painful sensation in your stomach that made you dizzy and weak, and never went away. Our hope was that there would be enough food to keep us alive until the next morning.

Our food was also not *food* as most people understand that word. *Food* in a concentration camp meant a foul-smelling bowl of watery soup and a piece of stale bread. Throughout the day, we were always looking for something more to eat. We were ready to eat anything. Guards stood by the garbage piles outside the inmate kitchen and shot any desperately hungry prisoner who dared to dig through the garbage for scraps.

The commandant of the Plaszow camp was a German officer named Amon Goeth (pronounced "Get"). We heard that Goeth had grown up in Vienna, the cultured capital of Austria, so we hoped he would be a reasonable man. He turned out to be just the opposite. He was horrible and inhuman.

Amon Goeth was six feet four inches tall, overweight, and brutal. Everyone in the camp knew his reputation and stayed as far away from him as possible. He lived in a villa on a hill about a hundred yards from the main gates of Plaszow. Each morning he stood on the balcony of his villa, aimed his rifle at people coming and going inside the camp, fired his gun, and killed prisoners at random.

My uncle Roman worked as a painter in Plaszow. One morning the guards put him to work painting one of the barracks. Amon Goeth came to inspect the work. He looked at the barrack, then drew his pistol and shot and killed my uncle. Roman had done nothing to provoke him. Goeth had no reason to kill my uncle other than his disdain for human life. Prisoners who had been in Plaszow for some time told us Goeth never ate his breakfast without shooting at least one person first. Killing made him happy.

Some days, Goeth forced us to witness prisoners being murdered. These poor people may have been guilty of some minor offense, such as stealing potato peels out of the garbage, but it didn't matter. They were Jews, and that was reason enough for Goeth to have the guards kill them. Life in the Krakow ghetto had been harsh, but that was nothing like what we saw in Plaszow, where every day Commandant Goeth committed terrible acts.

Thankfully, during that terrible year in Plaszow, I began hearing the name Oskar Schindler.

7.

SCHINDLER'S LIST

OSKAR SCHINDLER WAS A handsome German businessman who joined the Nazi Party in 1939. He was never particularly interested in politics. He liked expensive houses, fast cars, and opportunities to make money. After Germany invaded Poland in September 1939, he moved to Krakow, where the German authorities invited him to live in a big apartment previously owned by a Jewish family.

Oskar Schindler knew Krakow well. Before the war, he had worked for his father selling farm equipment, and business appointments frequently brought him to the city. Thanks to his contacts in business and government, Schindler received permission in 1940 to take over a factory located in a suburb of Krakow. He renamed his business the German Enamelware Factory—Emalia for short. Emalia was so close to the Krakow ghetto that Schindler made a deal with the German authorities to have Jews from the ghetto work for him.

At first, his reason for wanting Jewish workers was simple: They were cheaper than non-Jewish workers. Nazi policy declared that Jews were less than human, and the German government was happy to send him Jewish workers at a low price. Jewish workers also worked longer and harder than non-Jewish workers, since working meant they were useful and worth keeping alive.

Since Schindler's factory was located near the Krakow ghetto, he had witnessed how badly the Nazis treated Jews. For him, Jewish workers were not just cheap labor but also human beings—mothers, fathers, and children who were the innocent victims of Nazi cruelty.

The closing of the Krakow ghetto was a problem for Oskar Schindler. He depended on having his workers close by, and now they would be two miles away in the Plaszow camp. He had a choice. He could move his factory closer to Plaszow, or he could keep his factory where it was and build a small camp—a "subcamp"—where his workers could live. One day he approached Commandant Goeth and explained his idea for building a subcamp close to the Emalia factory.

"It's a waste of time for prisoners to walk two and a half miles from Plaszow," Schindler told Goeth. "It makes them tired and less productive. Let me build my own subcamp where workers can live. They will get to the factory faster each morning. I have orders to fill for the German government, and I need workers in the factory as many hours as possible each day. Besides, it will mean more money for me, and that will also be good for you."

Then Schindler slid a bag of diamonds across the table. Goeth put the bribe in his pocket and gave permission for Schindler to build his subcamp.

Bribes were an important but costly part of Oskar Schindler's business dealings. He was obliged to pay bribes to get permits to build his factory, win contracts from the German government, and maintain good relations with people on the black market who sold his pots and pans. The bribes included watches, cameras, saddles, boots, sports cars, diamonds, and lots of cash. Running a factory was costing him a fortune. This is important to know, because eventually Schindler decided to spend any available money on bribes to help keep his Jewish workers alive. That is what has earned him such a cherished place both in the history of the Holocaust and in the hearts of survivors like me.

In December 1943, my mother learned that Oskar Schindler needed more prisoners to work in his factory. She sent me to speak with the person who wrote the list of "Schindler Jews"—meaning those prisoners assigned to work at the Emalia factory—and I begged him to put me and my mother on the list. This person once shared our apartment in the Krakow ghetto and may have felt an obligation toward us. He put our names on the list, and that's how my mother and I became Schindler Jews. Soon after getting on the list, we moved into the Emalia subcamp.

The entrance to Schindler's factory was a wide metal gate. Inside the gate were two buildings. In one building, workers manufactured metal pots and pans that were then dipped in hot enamel and dried. In the other building, workers made armaments for the German army, mostly shell casings polished by hand. Past these two buildings was the subcamp, with watchtowers for the German guards, a kitchen, washrooms, a food-storage warehouse, offices, and barracks.

The first time I saw Oskar Schindler, he was smoking a cigarette and wearing an expensive suit. There was a diamond swastika on his lapel. The swastika was the sign of Nazi Germany, so for Jews it was the symbol of destruction and death. At that time, I didn't know much about him, just that he was a powerful person, but I learned that we had no need to be afraid of him.

There aren't enough words to describe Oskar's kindness to his workers. To protect us, he made sure no Nazi guards entered the factory without his permission. He purchased food for us on the black market. This meant we ate better and stayed healthier than less fortunate Jews in concentration camps, who were given nothing but rotten soup. While millions of Jews were being murdered elsewhere, the Jews working for Oskar Schindler survived. We had medicine when we were sick, water and soap to stay clean, and decent food to eat.

Each evening, Oskar announced that he needed some younger prisoners to clean his office. A group of us younger people would go to his office, lie down under the desks, and fall asleep. Oskar didn't really need help cleaning his office: It was a tactic, a way of providing his younger workers with an excuse for refreshing themselves with a good night's sleep.

I admired Oskar as he walked through his factory and stopped to talk with his workers, calling them by name. He left half-smoked cigarettes at various stations, pretending he forgot them when actually he was leaving them for men who had a smoking habit. I remember saying to myself, "God has sent an angel to save us." We were still prisoners, we still worked long hard days, and we were still hated by the Nazis—but for those of us lucky enough to work for Oskar, the Emalia factory was paradise.

<hr />

The factory operated round the clock, twenty-four hours a day. We worked in twelve-hour shifts. Some of the adults carried and worked with heavy metal supplies and other industrial materials, which was too dangerous for a thirteen-year-old like me. Instead, I worked on a little machine that made small-caliber bullet shells. The grown-ups worked on bigger machines that made larger shells. Operating these bigger machines involved pushing a heavy lever up and down. Everyone had trouble with that lever, which was always breaking. One day, the factory foreman took me off my little machine and put me to work on one of the bigger machines, and right away it broke. The foreman came over and expressed anger over the breakdown.

"You did this on purpose!" he yelled. "I'm going to get a guard to shoot you!"

Although I knew Oskar never allowed German guards to enter the factory unattended, let alone shoot anyone, I was terrified. One of the other workers ran to Oskar and told him what was going on. He came down from his office to the factory floor.

"What happened?" he asked. The foreman pointed at me and insisted I had broken the machine on purpose.

Oskar looked at little me and then at that big machine. "Don't ever put a little girl to work on such a big machine," he told the foreman. "Only men are allowed to work on that machine."

I was crying from fear. Oskar patted me on the head and said, "Don't worry. Where were you working before?" I showed him the smaller machine.

"That is where she should work," he instructed the foreman, "and that's where she should stay."

After that, whenever Oskar toured his factory, he stopped by my spot and asked, "How are you doing, little one?" He was like a father watching over me and over all the people working for him.

Then everything went terribly wrong.

8.

1944–

AUSCHWITZ

BY SUMMER OF 1944, Nazi Germany was starting to lose the war, thanks to constant attacks by American and British forces from the west and Soviet Russian forces from the east. The Germans knew that soon they would be held accountable for the torture and murders committed inside the camps. To hide their crimes, they began closing smaller camps such as Plaszow and deporting prisoners to camps west inside Germany.

Even though we worked for Oskar, we were still slaves of the Plaszow administrators, who put us to work helping close down the camp. Some of us were ordered to pack up stolen goods for shipment to Nazi headquarters in Berlin. These included gold watches, jewelry, silverware, paintings, and other possessions stolen from Jews. We placed these valuables in wooden crates, nailed the crates shut, and loaded them onto trucks and trains.

We watched in terror as the Jews from Plaszow were loaded onto trucks and trains and sent off to be killed. To give you an idea of how many were murdered, before the Germans closed the Plaszow camp, there were about eighteen thousand women prisoners. After they closed the camp, fewer than two thousand women prisoners remained, including me and my mother.

Oskar worried that his factory would be closed and his Jewish workers deported along with other prisoners to camps in Germany. Then he had an idea. It was risky, but he had always taken chances, and fortune often had been on his side. His idea was to dismantle the entire factory—equipment, machines, and supplies—load everything into boxcars, and relocate Emalia from Krakow, Poland, to Brünnlitz, Czechoslovakia, which is now called Brnenec, in the Czech Republic. There, near the town where he was born, he would reconstruct his factory and continue manufacturing ammunition. It took a lot of money to do this, because he had to bribe dozens of officials with expensive gifts to get the permits needed for such a move. But he succeeded.

Why did he go to so much trouble? One reason may have been selfish. He hoped that after the war he could rebuild his business in Czechoslovakia and continue making money. But another reason was unselfish. He knew the Nazis planned to murder as many Jews as possible before the Allies—meaning the American, British, and Russian armies—arrived. By relocating his factory, he hoped he could also relocate his Jewish workers and save their lives.

But even someone as influential as Oskar Schindler could not save us from all the horrors of the Holocaust, especially the terror known as Auschwitz.

In October 1944, guards marched me, my mother, and the other Schindler women to a train station and shoved us into boxcars. Guards shut the big wooden doors, and the train left the station. There was no water, food, bathroom, or windows, or even much oxygen, but we believed the train was taking us to Oskar's new factory in Czechoslovakia. So we tolerated the overcrowding, hunger, and foul smells as best we could.

After several hours, the train stopped. It was late at night. The doors opened, and a blinding spotlight hit our eyes. When our sight adjusted, we saw barbed-wire fences stretching in both directions. There was a terrible stench like rotting meat. German soldiers stood before us with rifles and dogs. I looked up and saw a sign that read AUSCHWITZ-BIRKENAU.

We had heard rumors about this place. It was said to be a killing center where Jews were murdered in gas chambers and their bodies burned in crematoria ovens. There must be a mistake, we told ourselves. We worked for Oskar Schindler. Why were we in Auschwitz?

"Everyone off the train!" guards yelled. "*Raus!* Quickly!"

The guards beat us with whips and made us jump down onto the arrival platform. White flakes like snow were falling all around us. We were thirsty after traveling so long without water and stuck out our tongues to catch the flakes, but they didn't taste like snow. We looked up and realized the flakes were falling from tall chimneys above the crematoria ovens. White ashes. Human ashes.

My mother and I watched a German officer sort us into groups of those who were physically healthy and those who were not. He sent the strong women to the right and the weak or sickly women to the left. To make ourselves look healthier, we copied other women around us and pinched our cheeks until they were rosy. When our turn came, the guard looked us over and sent us to the right. We learned later that the weaker people in the left line went immediately to die in the gas chambers.

Guards marched our group inside a barrack and told us to strip naked. We stood huddled together, shivering. What happened next was humiliating. Male prisoners wearing striped uniforms used rusty scissors and razor blades to shave off all our hair. The equipment was old and dull and tugged painfully on our hair, and many of us began to cry.

When I was little, I had beautiful thick braids. In the Krakow ghetto, my mother had cut my hair short so it would be easier to keep clean. But a shaved head? That moment was the first time I felt as if I was losing my identity. I didn't feel like myself anymore.

The women around me huddled together and shook like leaves from cold and fear. I thought, "Who can look like this and still be alive?" I stared up at the woman next to me and could hardly believe this bald person was my mother. Then guards pushed us into a dark room, yelling, "Plaszow scum! We shouldn't be wasting our time with you!"

I looked up and noticed metal pipes with small holes, crisscrossing the ceiling. We had no idea where we were or what this room was. We had heard rumors of people dying in gas chambers, but who could believe such a nightmare? We had no idea what would happen to us. All at once, something came out of the pipes and we held our breath. It was water. We weren't going to die that day.

———◆◆◆———

The cold shower ended, and women guards chased us out of the room with sticks. They pointed to piles of wooden shoes and ordered us to take one pair each. Then they pointed to a pile of clothes and yelled again to quickly get dressed. People grabbed whatever they could put their hands on. I saw a yellow dress with red flowers and tried to put it on, but it was huge, made for a heavy, tall woman, not a skinny fifteen-year-old. I tied the dress around my waist as best I could. Then they pushed us outside.

This was late autumn 1944. The weather was cold and it had been raining. Guards marched us down a muddy road and into a barrack, where we collapsed on wooden bunks covered with a thin layer of smelly straw. There wasn't enough room for everyone, so some of the women lay down on the stone floor. The women in charge of our barracks were Hungarian. We didn't speak their language, and because we had no idea what they were saying, they would beat us for not obeying instructions.

How did it feel to be yelled at in a foreign language, beaten with sticks, and not know what we were supposed to do? How did it feel to be starving and not knowing if we were going to live one more day? How did it feel to be surrounded by prisoners who looked more dead than alive? It felt like the Nazis had taken away my soul.

9.

LIVING IN A NIGHTMARE

WORDS HAVE NOT BEEN invented to describe Auschwitz. Being there meant starving, getting sicker every day, and seeing things your eyes had trouble believing. Let me try to describe something of this horrible place.

Of the more than forty thousand camps built by the Nazis, Auschwitz was not only the largest concentration camp, but also the largest killing center. Auschwitz, which was divided into three main camps, was located approximately forty-one miles west of Krakow, where I was born. There was the main camp, called Auschwitz I. Two miles from the main camp was Auschwitz-Birkenau, also called Auschwitz II, where deportation trains rolled in day and night. And there was Auschwitz-Monowitz, also known as Auschwitz III, where prisoners worked in factories day and night.

During six years of operation, between 1.1 and 1.3 million people were murdered in Auschwitz: Jews, Sinti and Roma people (once called Gypsies), Soviet prisoners of war, political prisoners, and other people labeled by the Nazis as "antisocials." Nine out of every ten people murdered in Auschwitz were Jews.

One morning, two officers took me and another girl out of the roll-call line and marched us to a clinic some distance away. Inside the clinic, a nurse had us lie on beds with white sheets. "Don't be afraid," she told us. "After this, you will be brought back to your barrack."

She inserted a needle in our arms, drew blood, and told us something strange. "The blood will be used to save wounded German soldiers," she said. Can you imagine? The Germans made up lies about Jews being less than human, but it seemed our blood was good enough to save their soldiers.

When she was finished taking our blood, the nurse handed us each a piece of bread with a slice of liverwurst on it. It was the best food we had seen in a long time and I was hungry, but I only took a bite and saved the rest for my mother. When guards brought us back to our barrack, I told my mother what had happened. She insisted I eat the rest of the bread and liverwurst myself.

We worked all day, digging ditches, carrying supplies, and doing whatever the Germans told us to do. Sometimes at night, guards marched me and some other girls to the kitchen. They put wooden poles across our shoulders, and at both ends of the pole they hung heavy buckets of smelly soup made with potato peels and sawdust. They pushed us out the door and forced us to carry the buckets down muddy roads to the barracks, where prisoners stood in line to receive a little bit of the rotten soup. For many, it was their only "meal" of the day.

My image of the German people before the war was that they were just like people everywhere: teachers, bus drivers, plumbers, electricians—normal people, fathers and mothers, brothers and sisters. Maybe many of them didn't like Jews, but they were still human and we were all part of the same human race.

Auschwitz destroyed that image. People who previously were respectable, law-abiding citizens became murderers and took part in the massacre of hundreds, thousands, and then millions of human beings, solely because they were Jews. How could that happen?

How great is our responsibility to make sure it never happens again?

———◆◆◆———

When Oskar learned that we, his women workers, had been sent to Auschwitz, he was furious. We were never supposed to be sent there. It appeared that a clerical error was about to erase all his efforts to keep us alive. To secure our release, he negotiated by phone with Auschwitz commandant Rudolf Hoess (pronounced "Hess"). Then Oskar sent his secretary to meet Hoess in person.

"These women are experts at their jobs," the secretary explained to Hoess. "They are highly trained and irreplaceable. I'm sure we can come to an agreement to have them sent back to the factory."

The secretary then put a bag of precious diamonds on the table. Hoess pocketed the diamonds and signed a sheet of paper giving permission for the

Schindler Jews to be shipped out. Oskar had again saved us from destruction.

The secretary handed the commandant a list of all the women who should be sent to the Emalia factory in Czechoslovakia, and within hours we were marched to the railway station and once more pushed into cattle cars. The guards shut the big wooden doors and the train departed. We had been in Auschwitz only three and a half weeks, but it was long enough that most of us were sick and starving. One of the girls in the cattle car was burning from a high fever. She lay her head in my lap. I put my fingers through a hole in the side of the boxcar, grabbed a few snowflakes, and rubbed them on her lips.

Hours later the train stopped and the doors opened. We were in Brünnlitz, Czechoslovakia. There on the platform stood Oskar, wearing his fancy green Tyrolean hat. We were so weak and embarrassed, we just sat there staring at him, amazed to still be alive. We smelled terrible, had lice in our hair and clothes, and looked like skeletons. Yet he seemed happy to see us.

"Well," he said with a smile, "here you are. There is hot soup ready for you. Your men are already here—your fathers, husbands, and brothers. I will take care of you. You have nothing to worry about." We looked at one another in disbelief. It was a miracle.

Hunger and the horrors of Auschwitz had made us weak. We climbed down from the cattle car as best we could and slowly walked the short distance from the train station to the factory. It was not as big or impressive as the factory Oskar had owned in Plaszow, but it looked like heaven to us: a place where we would be fed and sheltered.

Oskar brought us to a building, and we climbed the stairs to the workers' living quarters on the second floor. A wall running through the middle of the large room created separate spaces for men and women. It was here that my mother and I were reunited with my grandfather. At seventy-five years of age, he was the oldest person to have made it onto Schindler's list and the oldest person working in the Brünnlitz factory.

"I know you went through hell to get here," Oskar told us. "That is in the past now. We have doctors who will show you where to wash and who will take care of those of you who are sick."

In the basement of the factory, Oskar's wife, Emilie, had built a clinic for sick and wounded workers. She instructed the doctors, who came from the prisoner population, to bathe us and rub disinfectant powder over us to get rid of the lice. This was important, because lice carried deadly diseases, such as typhus. After three days in the clinic, we were free of the lice. Often I have thought back on those days and marveled at how Mrs. Schindler was like her husband: not a "good Nazi" but a good person.

By using his influence and wealth, Oskar rescued nearly 1,200 Jewish men and women. These were people who, thanks to him, escaped the fate of the other 25,000 men, women, and children of Plaszow who were sent to their deaths in the gas chambers of Auschwitz and other death camps. He performed this miracle just in time. One day more in Auschwitz and we, too, would have been killed.

These days, when I speak with students, someone will ask me, "Why didn't you try to escape?" It's a good question, but how could Jews during the Holocaust escape when there were machine guns pointed at them and patrol dogs ready to pounce? Besides, there was no place to escape to. All around the camps were non-Jews who hated us and who were cooperating with the Nazis to murder us all. Some people did try to escape, young people in particular who had the strength to run away. A handful succeeded. But if any of the non-Jews living near the camps saw them, they called the police. The police hunted them down and shot them on the spot.

For those of us so fortunate to work for Oskar, we never thought about running away. I will give you another example of how well he cared for us. Oskar and Emilie owned a villa located close to their Brünnlitz factory, but Oskar knew we were terrified the Germans would arrest us during the night and send us to our deaths. To calm our fears, he never slept in his beautiful villa. Instead, he slept in a small office on the ground floor of his factory, keeping watch over us. For nine months, up to the day we were liberated by the Russians, my mother and I led a sheltered and protected life under his care.

Emilie deserves just as much appreciation as her husband. If any of us were sick, she took care of us. She went to the nearby village to look for extra food and find farina cereal to cook for younger ones like me. She outfitted the clinic with medical equipment purchased on the black market.

Some of the prisoners were already dying when we

arrived at the Brünnlitz factory. One was an older woman who succumbed to a heart attack. The other was a young girl who died of cancer. Oskar and Emilie arranged for them to receive a proper Jewish burial in a secret graveyard behind the factory. They even noted the spot where these women were buried so that, after the war, their bodies could be found and relocated to a Jewish cemetery. Such kindness toward Jews was illegal under German law, but the Schindlers didn't care.

We knew how lucky we were. For every Jew saved by Oskar and Emilie, there were tens of thousands who did not survive.

<hr />

One cold day toward the end of January 1945, Oskar and Emilie learned that a train carrying prisoners had stopped at a nearby station. The boxcars were rumored to be filled with Jewish slave laborers from a factory named Golleschau (pronounced

"Go-lesh-ow"), a subcamp of Auschwitz. When the Russian army approached from the east, the Germans closed down the Golleschau factory and transported the Jewish laborers by train to a smaller camp in Czechoslovakia. But the train was delayed for more than a week, and all the while ninety-six Jewish prisoners were locked in freezing boxcars without food or water.

Years later, Emilie explained what happened next. The locks on the boxcar doors had frozen shut. When the locks were cut and the doors opened, the scene was "a nightmare almost beyond imagination," Emilie wrote in her memoir. Thirteen of the prisoners in the boxcar had died, but the others were still breathing.

The Schindlers brought all the prisoners still alive to their clinic, and Emilie worked around the clock to try to save them. In the morning, she went to the train station with suitcases full of vodka.

When trains arrived, she traded the vodka for as many medical supplies as she could get from train passengers, then brought the supplies back to the clinic.

Next to the Schindlers' factory was a grain mill run by a family named Daubek. Emilie went to see Mrs. Daubek and explained that grain from the mill was desperately needed. "I want to see that our Jewish workers don't starve to death," Emilie explained. Mrs. Daubek agreed to help, and Emilie returned to the factory with sacks of grains and semolina flour. In the clinic, she carefully fed her patients from the Golleschau train. After not eating for so long, they could digest only one spoonful of porridge at a time. Eventually, thanks to her care, most of them regained their health.

Those of us who survived the Holocaust as Schindler Jews remember Mrs. Schindler with as much gratitude as we do her husband, Oskar.

Meanwhile, Oskar continued to spend all his money buying food to keep us alive. He also had to feed more than a hundred German officers who were assigned to guard his factory. To keep the officers friendly, he gave them expensive alcohol and cigarettes. All of us working in his factory wondered the same thing: How much longer would his money last? And what would happen to us when it ran out?

10.

1944-45—

WAR'S END

BY JANUARY 18, 1945, it was clear that Germany was about to lose the war, and the Nazis decided the time had come to murder all remaining Jewish prisoners. We learned later what happened to the prisoners in Auschwitz. Guards lined them up in front of the gates and force-marched them to camps in Germany and Austria. This was one of the worst winters in history, with temperatures dropping to

30 degrees below zero. About sixty thousand prisoners departed in columns five across, long lines of miserable, freezing human beings, made to walk for their lives—death marches, as they were called.

For days, prisoners marched through the piercing cold and snow. Whoever was too exhausted to continue walking was shot and left to die by the side of the road.

That would have been our fate if not for Oskar. While other prisoners were freezing and starving, we were safe inside his factory.

But now Oskar was in trouble. The Russian forces coming to liberate the camps would not see him as a hero, the way we did. They would see him as a Nazi businessman who manufactured ammunition for the German army and had concentration-camp prisoners working for him. He would surely be made to stand trial and possibly be hanged for war crimes.

The time had come for him to flee. In May 1945, with Russian soldiers only a day away, Oskar called for all his workers and all the German guards to gather in the factory.

First he spoke to us.

"My children," he said, "you are saved. Germany has lost the war." He then asked that we not go into the neighboring houses to steal anything. "Prove yourself worthy of the millions of victims among you and refrain from any individual acts of revenge and terror," he said.

Then he turned to the Nazi guards and began by thanking them for being humane toward his workers. It was a good strategy to compliment them, because they were Nazi soldiers and quite capable of killing us all before the Russians arrived.

"You have a choice," he told the Germans. "You can stay here, wait for the Russians, and be arrested for war crimes, or you can leave now and return to your families." The choice was simple. Since no one from the German government was there to stop them from leaving, they all turned and walked out of the factory.

Then Oskar performed one last act of generosity for his Jewish workers. To each worker, he gave a bottle of vodka, a pair of shoes, and three yards of fabric. These rare goods would bring a high price on the black market, and the money would buy us food on our journey home to Krakow.

We gave him a gift in return: a ring made from a gold tooth donated by one of the Jewish workers, and a letter of appreciation that spelled out his many acts of kindness toward us. Then we all formed a line, walked up one by one, and kissed the hands of Oskar and Emilie Schindler. Everyone wept to see them leave.

"I wish I could have done more," he said, "but I must leave you now. *Auf Wiedersehen*—goodbye."

Oskar and Emilie drove away. Eventually, they succeeded in reaching the area where American troops were in charge. Because the Americans were arresting all the Nazis they could find, our letter of appreciation helped the Schindlers avoid prison.

By May 8, 1945, when Germany surrendered to the Allies, many former Nazis had fled and were living comfortably in hiding. Meanwhile, Oskar had spent all his money to save his workers, and now he was in need of help. For a while, all that he and Emilie had to live on were monthly CARE packages. *CARE* stood for the Cooperative for American Remittances to Europe, an agency that sent food relief to people at risk of starving at the end of World War II.

CARE packages typically contained cans of meat, bags of powdered eggs, boxes of preserves, margarine, sugar, powdered milk, and coffee. Living on such charity was a difficult adjustment for the Schindlers, who had once been wealthy.

Eventually, the Jewish community found out that the man who had saved more than a thousand Jews was himself in need, and leaders of Jewish relief organizations realized they had to do something to help him. Germany was not safe for Oskar, who was attacked in the streets as a Jew lover. In 1949, Jewish organizations arranged for Oskar and Emilie to relocate to Argentina, where there were business opportunities and where they could start life anew.

For a while, Oskar tried to open a factory in Argentina, but his health was not good and the business failed. In 1957, he went back to Germany, where the Jewish community supported him with monthly checks. In 1964, he suffered a heart attack. His health never recovered.

After the war, when the deaths were added up, it was discovered that from 1933, when Hitler became chancellor of Germany, to 1945, when the war ended, the Nazis had murdered more than six million Jews. Who can even imagine such a number? Six million innocent men, women, and children—a tragedy so great it has come to be known as "history's darkest hour."

During those terrible years, some Christians had taken immense risks to help save Jews, and in the 1950s the government of Israel awarded these good people the title Righteous Gentiles. Oskar Schindler had not started out in life righteously. He drank and smoked, he enjoyed the company of women, and his goal in Krakow in the early days of the war was simply to make money.

Yet over time he changed. He wanted to save his workers, and to do so, he spent all his money bribing German officials and purchasing food and medicine. He risked his life and went broke to save me and more than a thousand other Jewish prisoners. Before he died in 1974 at age sixty-six, he asked to be buried in Jerusalem, the holiest of cities for

Jews. Emilie died in Germany in 2001 at age ninety-four.

In 1993, the government of Israel recognized Oskar and Emilie Schindler as Righteous Gentiles.

11.

RETURN TO A
DANGEROUS CITY

NOW I WILL TELL you what happened to me and my mother. The day after Oskar and Emilie drove away, a Russian soldier on horseback rode up to the factory. He called out to us, "You are free!" Were we really free? Survivors will tell you that they will never be free from the terrible memories of what they went through: the starvation, torture, humiliation, and murder of so many innocent people.

Each of us reacted differently to our liberation.

Some chose to walk home to Krakow more than two hundred miles away. Others, including my mother and me, decided to wait until the Russians could arrange for a train to take us home. Near the Emalia factory in Brünnlitz, my mother and I found a little cottage that had been abandoned by its Czech owners. We stayed there for a few days until word reached us that a train was ready to take us to Krakow.

At the Brünnlitz station, friendly Russian soldiers helped us climb into boxcars. There were maybe 150 of us finally on our way home. The train was not like the terrible one that had brought us to Auschwitz. In this one, the soldiers had kindly provided wooden beds with blankets and food and water.

"When you get back to Krakow," the soldiers warned us, "don't go outside at night. Some Polish people don't want you there, and there could be trouble." After all we had been through, we had hoped that people in Krakow would be sympathetic and welcome us home. That did not happen. Anti-Semitism was still strong in Poland, and we would have to be careful.

After two days, the train arrived. People at the train station told us there was a refugee agency set up to help Jews returning to Krakow. We walked to the agency's address, a building that had previously been a school. We were hoping to be assigned a place to live and to find news of our family. The walls of the office were covered with messages on pieces of paper: "My name is so-and-so; do you know anyone from my family?" We did not find our names anywhere. No one here was looking for us, not any of my father's six brothers or their wives or children, not any of my grandparents, cousins, aunts, or uncles. Eventually, I found two of my eleven cousins who were still alive, as well as my father's sister. No one else from our family had survived.

A Russian official told us we could stay in a college dormitory that had been converted into a shelter, but my mother didn't want us to live like that anymore, with strangers crowded into one room. First we wondered if we could move back into our old apartment, so we walked from the station to our street, entered our building, and climbed the stairs.

When we got to the apartment, we discovered someone had moved in. He told us he was a lawyer, and because the landlord didn't know if we were ever going to come home, he had been allowed to rent the apartment from the time we left. We were not surprised to find someone living in our place. We had no hard feelings about it and didn't blame him for moving into our apartment. How was he supposed to know we would survive?

The apartment was very much as we had left it in 1941 when we were forced to move into the Krakow ghetto. The same color paint was on the walls, and the same lamps were hanging from the ceiling. The same linoleum covered the floor, and my parents' clothes closet and wooden bench were still there. But we didn't stay long. The apartment was no longer our home. We had to find a new place to live.

The fabric, shoes, and vodka given to us by Oskar proved useful. We were able to sell these items, so there was some money for food and rent. Eventually, we found an apartment to rent, although it wasn't nice. I had to pour hot water onto the mattress to get rid of its bedbugs. But at least it was our own place, and that was a lucky thing.

As the Russian soldiers had warned us, many people were not happy about Jews returning to Krakow. On several occasions they tricked Jews by telling them, "You can sleep here tonight," and during the night they murdered them.

We stayed in Krakow a month or so, but life there was too dangerous. Every day, there were outbursts of anti-Semitism. How strange to return to the place where I had grown up, a place I had loved, only to realize it would never be the same again. The streets of Krakow were stained with Jewish blood. The Jewish population was all but gone, murdered by the Nazis. Krakow was no longer a place where we could rebuild our lives, and my mother and I looked for somewhere else to go.

A girl I had known before the war heard we were back and came to visit. We described for her how uncomfortable we felt in Krakow and how much we wanted to find some other place to live.

"Many Jewish survivors have gone to Austria," she said, "to live in a displaced persons camp—a DP camp. I hear it's comfortable there, and Jews don't have to worry about being attacked. Why not try there?"

My mother and I agreed that this sounded like a good plan. Just as we were about to leave for the DP camp in Linz, Austria, we had another visitor. This time, it was a boy who had been our neighbor in the Krakow ghetto.

"Rena, I have a surprise for you," he said. "Your friend Sonia from the Krakow ghetto is alive. She and her sister and brother-in-law are all living on a farm not far from the DP camp where you are going. I will take you to her."

In the days after the end of the war, camp survivors were allowed to ride trains and buses for free. When at last we arrived in Linz and found our way to the farm, Sonia and I fell into each other's arms and wept like babies. We wept for the murder of her parents. We wept for the murder of my father. We wept for all the innocent Jewish men, women, and children who had been murdered.

When we had shed all the tears we could, we fell back into our old ways of talking about everything, about boys and food, and laughing like we used to do to chase away the sadness.

In Linz, I found a job as a typist and translator for the United Nations Relief and Rehabilitation Administration (UNRRA), an agency that provided food, shelter, and other necessities to victims of the war. Sonia found a job with the Hebrew Immigrant Aid Society (HIAS), an organization that provided humanitarian aid and assistance to refugees. We earned some money and swore to never be separated again.

In Linz, I also met my future husband.

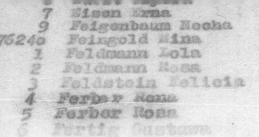

12.

Marriage and America

BY JULY 1945, THE American army had set up offices in Linz for the U.S. Army Counter Intelligence Corps (the CIC), which was responsible for tracking down Nazis who ran away at the end of the war. Anyone who worked for the CIC had the special privilege of shopping at the Army PX (Post Exchange), which sold hard-to-find food, spices, and other items not available in the public markets. One day a friend came running to see me and Sonia at the farm. She was excited.

"I spent time with some boys working with the CIC," she said. "You have to meet them. They have cans of fruit and milk!"

Sonia and I were teenagers and a bit mischievous. "Why not?" we answered, and off we went to Linz.

Our mutual friend introduced me to a twenty-four-year-old man from Krakow named Marek, who worked for the CIC. He was an educated young man who had been liberated from the Mauthausen concentration camp. Marek spoke English well, and the Americans were glad to have him work for them as a translator. He looked handsome in his American uniform. We had a lovely dinner, and Marek came back to visit me again the next day—and the day after that, and the day after that.

In years to come, Marek would tell our children that it was "love at first sight," and that he used a lasso to capture me. There was no lasso, but I would agree that it was love at first sight. We married and could not have been happier. The only thing missing was a way to move to America.

———◆◆◆———

Sonia had a relative who lived in Massachusetts and who was willing to sponsor Marek and me. That meant the relative was willing to provide a letter saying that, if necessary, he would cover our living expenses in the United States and guarantee that we would not become dependent on charity. Thanks to that letter, Marek and I arrived in America by steamship on November 19, 1948.

The first thing we did was look for work. Marek found a job in a leather factory, and I worked as an assistant in a shoe factory. It was not the life I had dreamed of as a girl, but we were alive, in America, and had nothing to complain about.

Six years later, I was able to send papers for my mother and her new husband, who was also a

Holocaust survivor, to come from Europe to America. By then, Marek and I had three children. My mother and her husband found jobs and bought a house. We were all so happy to be a family together again.

My dear friend Sonia had immigrated to the United States a few months before me, along with her sister and brother-in-law. I spoke with her about whether we should tell people about our experiences, and at first we decided not to. It would be too painful to discuss publicly, and besides, we also knew nobody wanted to hear such horrible things.

Then something happened that made us change our minds. People known as Holocaust deniers were declaring that the Holocaust never happened, and that Jews invented the Holocaust to win people's sympathy. Sonia and I agreed something had to be done about Holocaust denial. The best thing we could do would be to speak the truth about what we had personally endured. But we weren't sure how to go about it.

Then, in 1979, we met a remarkable woman named Margot.

Margot Stern Strom grew up in Memphis, Tennessee, in the 1940s and 1950s. Back then, Memphis was segregated, and from the window of her high school, Margot could see a sign in the zoo across the street that said Thursdays were "Colored Day Only"—the only day of the week that African Americans were allowed to visit the zoo. Later in life, Margot recounted that during her childhood, people didn't talk about racism, anti-Semitism, or the Holocaust. Discrimination and bigotry were just the way things had always been, and nobody seemed willing to do anything about it.

Margot became a teacher and devoted her career to educating young people about injustice. In 1976, she cofounded an organization called Facing History and Ourselves, which today has taught millions of students and teachers about the Holocaust and the causes of prejudice. Facing History and Ourselves has grown into an international network of more than forty thousand educators who reach four million students in more than two hundred countries every year.

My dear friend Sonia was the first one to work with Margot in classrooms. By then, Sonia was married and had three wonderful children, yet she found time to meet with students, tell them of her experiences, and answer their questions about the Holocaust.

I remember the first time Margot invited me to speak to a group of students. Their teacher was nervous, because one of the parents had found out about my talk and told Margot, "I don't want my child to learn about the Holocaust."

Who could blame her? What sensitive parent

wants her child to hear about starvation and murder? This parent felt better when Margot explained that my message was not so much about atrocities as about how everyone, including young people, can make a difference in the world.

Sonia died from cancer in 2010, and her death was a terrible loss for me. It was, and it still is. What kind of world is this, I wondered, where someone can survive the Holocaust and then die of cancer? Is there no justice at all? Then I remembered something important about Sonia that helped me out of my depression. She was never bitter, despite all she had gone through. Remembering that didn't erase the sadness of losing her, but it helped me to recall that she and I always shared the same philosophy: Life, however long or short, is a blessing.

When I remember that, Sonia is still with me.

13.

The Movie

SCHINDLER'S LIST

FOR MANY YEARS AFTER the war, there had been talk about making the true story of Oskar Schindler into a movie. The first person to write a book about him was an Australian author named Thomas Keneally, whose novel *Schindler's Ark* was published in 1982. The famous director Steven Spielberg (who made such films as *E.T.*, *Jurassic Park*, and the Indiana Jones series) turned the Keneally book into a movie in 1993 called *Schindler's List*. The response world-wide was astonishing. *Schindler's List* received twelve Academy Award nominations, won seven of the twelve nominations, and became one of the most acclaimed films of all time.

The first time I saw *Schindler's List*, I felt like I had gone inside the movie and was a part of history once again. There on the screen was Oskar Schindler, played by actor Liam Neeson. There on the screen were other actors, portraying Emilie Schindler and many people I had known back then. It was astonishing to see my own story brought to life.

The film was so powerful that it took me back to my childhood when the Nazis took over Krakow, back to the day we were forced into the ghetto, and back into the Plaszow camp, where we did not know from one moment to the next if we would live or die. The film put me back inside Auschwitz, where we lived every moment in terror, and left me numb. When it ended, I sat in my seat without even knowing it was over.

Someone tapped me on my shoulder and asked, "Are you ready to leave now?" I looked around. The theater was empty. Everyone had already left, and I was the last person there. The movie had over-powered me to the point that I had lost track of where I was.

Many young people get their impressions of history from films such as *Schindler's List*, and that's important because we need to remember the Holocaust. At the same time, real history is always more complicated than what we see in movies. There are things survivors won't talk about, things you could never show on a screen. Who wants to pay money to see a film about the terrible things people had to do just to stay alive?

Movies also follow rules of drama and storytelling. Actual events are not usually so predictable, and people who make movies often change details to make the story more interesting. This raises an important question. Which history is the real history? Is it the history we read in books? The history we see in movies? The history told by survivors? Survivors' memories sometimes change over time. Whose version is the real version? You might like to discuss this in one of your classes.

14.

CLOSING THOUGHTS

DURING THOSE TERRIBLE YEARS when millions of Jews and others suffered and died under Nazi rule, many government leaders around the world knew what was happening. People who had escaped from concentration camps brought evidence of the atrocities—firsthand reports, sometimes even photographs—but government leaders chose to do nothing. "There's nothing we can do for the Jews," they said. "We have to concentrate on winning the war."

With all due respect to these leaders, could there have been some anti-Semitism on their part? Such prejudice against others because of religion, race, or skin color must stop. The late President John F. Kennedy once said, "If we cannot end now our differences, at least we can help make the world safe for diversity. For, in the final analysis, our most basic common link is that we all inhabit this small planet. We all breathe the same air. We all cherish our children's future. And we are all mortal."

Over the many years I have been speaking in public, mainly to students, my message is always the same: You don't have to love everyone, but everyone deserves to be treated fairly. Genocide starts when some people think they are better than others. "It is those others," they say, "who are the cause of all bad things happening in the world. They don't deserve fair treatment. They deserve to die."

That was Hitler's message. He may be gone, but that terrible belief lives on wherever people are oppressed. So when you see a bully, do something. Go get help. Three kids willing to stand up to one bully can stop the bully cold. You can make a difference, not just in school but in the entire nation. In just a few years, I tell young people, you will be old enough to vote. That will give you the power to make a big difference in society.

As the years go by, I have shared that message in classes where the teachers themselves were once students I had spoken to. Now those teachers are passing the message along to their students. Perhaps one day their students will become teachers and pass the message along to yet another generation.

And perhaps you, too, dear reader, will be one of those with the courage to stand up for the innocent. Be an upstander, not a bystander.

ACKNOWLEDGMENTS

I want to thank Joshua M. Greene for taking on this project with such patience and care. Thanks also to my dear friend Judi Bohn, who provided important help and recommendations. Professor Lawrence Langer, one of the world's leading scholars of Holocaust witness testimony, generously gave suggestions for expanding the range of topics discussed here. My editor, Roy Wandelmaier, has given this book much personal attention, and I am grateful to him. Finally, I extend my appreciation to Steven Spielberg. Once his movie *Schindler's List* was seen around the world, the wall of silence came down and we survivors, along with the liberation soldiers who saved us from the camps and were also witnesses to the horror, were finally able to share our stories.

IN 1945, after the end of World War II, my mother and I returned to Krakow, Poland, where I was born. We went to the ghetto—the crowded section of the city where German soldiers had forced Jews to relocate in 1941—and entered the apartment where my grandparents once lived. The door to their apartment was wide open.

We didn't expect to find anything of value. All the furniture, linens, and silver had been stolen long ago. But in the attic, I found pictures of my family scattered about. Someone had taken my grandparents' lovely leather-bound albums and tossed away the images.

Many of the following photos were among those I was able to salvage from the attic floor.

Rena was born in Krakow, Poland, in 1929. Here is a photo of her at age five.

Young Rena (standing on the right) on a summer vacation before the war with her mother, Rosa (standing behind her), her father, Moses, and her father's sister Cyla (sitting).

In this photograph from 1939, Jewish people in Krakow, Poland, are being forced to build the walls of what would become the Krakow Ghetto, where the Jewish community would be forced to live.

The train tracks leading to Auschwitz.

Oskar Schindler (pictured here after the war).

lfd.Nr.	Art	H.Nr.	Name und Vorname	Geburts-datum	Beruf
1.	Jü.Po.	7620l	Aftergut Berta	20. 2.16	Metallarbeiterin
2.	"	2	Appel Gisela	28. 7.21	"
3.	"	3	Ast Rachela	20. 8.20	"
4.	"	4	Bamoh Lola	3. 7.08	"
5.	"	5	Barth Helena	25.12.10	"
6.	"	6	Begleiter Valeria	18. 5.21	Sanitäterin
7.	"	7.	Berger Hilde	13. 6.14	Schreibkraft
8.	"	8	Berhang Elka	7. 4.15	Metallarbeiterin
9.	"	9	Bernstein Golda	10.11.21	"
10.	"	7621o	Bielfeld Frania	31.3. 22	"
11.	"	1	Blawat Felicia	25.12.24	"
12.	"	2	Bernstein Henja Malka	29. 8.19	"
13.	"	3	Borger Anna	8. 3.15	"
14.	"	4	Blaszukrans Karola	19. 1.14	"
15.	"	5	Brenner Jetti	27. 8.13	Schreibkraft
16.	"	6	Brunngraber Helina	12. 3.26	Metallarbeiterin
17.	"	7	Brzeska Cecilia	24.12.26	"
18.	"	8	Brzeska Hela	10. 5.25	"
19.	"	9	Buchsbaum Sofia	11. 3.13	"
20.	"	7622o	Bernstein Basia	20. 4.26	"
21.	"	1	Brandsilber Charlotte	5. 4.09	"
22.	"	2	Brechzer Nelli	14. 5.86	"
23.	"	3	Breit Gisa	11. 8.11	"
24.	"	4	Bugajer Rachela	3. 2.18	"
25.	"	5	Burstiner Hela	27. 1.09	"
26.	"	7	Danzig Sara	26. 7.07	"
27.	Jü.Po.	8	Davidovicz Ida	6. 2.99	"
28.	Jü.Po.	9	Dortheimer Helena	19. 5.22	"
29.	"	7623o	Dortheimer Helena	8. 7.10	"
30.	"	1	Dressler Marta	11. 5.86	"
31.	"	2	Dressler Susi	1.10.14	Schneiderin
32.	"	3	Dresner Chaja	8. 4.05	Metallarbeiterin
33.	"	4	Dresner Danuta	24. 8.27	"
34.	"	5	Duklauer Anna	29.12.22	"
35.	"	6	Durst Sapira	3. 4.14	"
36.	"	7	Eisen Anna	27. 2.19	"
37.	"	9	Feigenbaum Necha	15. 1.02	"
38.	"	7624o	Feingold Nina	17. 7.10	"
39.	"	1	Feldmann Lola	1. 6.22	"
40.	"	2	Feldmann Rosa	4. 9.26	"
41.	"	3	Feldstein Felicia	10.14.24	"
42.	"	4	Ferber Rena	24. 2.28	"
43.	"	5	Ferber Rosa	14. 9.05	"
44.	"	6	Fertig Gustawa	21.12.22	"
45.	"	7	Feuereisen Eleonora	12. 6.24	"
46.	"	8	Finder Fela	15. 8.09	"
47.	"	9	Frey Cecilia	11.11.21	"
48.	"	7625o	Fröhlich Rosa	1. 3.15	"
49.	"	1	Fränkel Frieda	14. 4.24	"
50.	"	2	Friedmann Eugenia	16. 6.23	"
51.	"	3	Friedmann Estera	1.12.20	"
52.	"	4	Friedmann Felicia	2.1. 23	"
53.	"	5	Friedmann Helene	3. 9.04	"
54.	"	6	Friedner Franciska	5. 7.06	"
55.	"	7	Friedner Ada	15. 1.21	"
56.	"	8	Frisch Stefania	29. 4.27	"
57.	"	9	Frisch Ella	4. 3.03	"
58.	"	7626o	Gans Genia	1. 9.14	"
59.	"	1	Garde Mina	7. 8.99	"
60.	"	2	Garde Irena	2. 4.18	"

Schindler's List. Note the names of Rena and her mother (Rena and Rosa Ferber).

Rena at seventeen years old, when she was living in the Bindermichel Displaced Persons Camp after the war.

Rena with her husband, Mark Finder, on their wedding day.

In 1997, Rena and Mark visited Oskar Schindler's grave in Jerusalem with their grandchildren Jason and Amy.

Rena is dedicated to sharing her experiences during the Holocaust, and about the need to always speak out against injustice.

PHOTO CREDITS

If you would like to learn more about the Holocaust, here is another book you may be interested in.

Signs of Survival: A Memoir of the Holocaust by Renee Hartman and Joshua M. Greene is the true story of two sisters, one deaf and one hearing, who must fight to stay alive after their parents are captured by the Nazis.

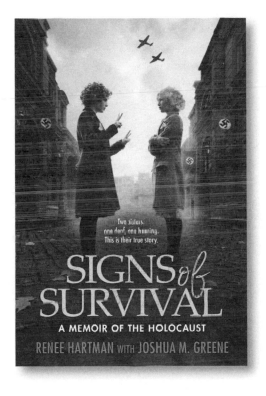

Read on for an excerpt.

1

The Sound of Boots

RENEE: IN 1943, GERMAN soldiers rounded up the Jews living in my city, Bratislava, and sent them to death camps to be killed. There would be eight to twelve soldiers marching together from house to house, knocking on doors, and yelling, "Get ready to leave! You have one hour!" I remember the stomping of their boots on the cobblestoned streets.

My parents, younger sister, and I lived in a fourth-floor apartment, and when I heard the sound of those boots, I ran to warn my family. Then we rushed into a room at the back of the apartment and hid. When the soldiers knocked on our door, we didn't answer and stayed as quiet as possible.

I was ten years old then, and my sister was eight. The responsibility was on me to warn everyone when the soldiers were coming because my sister and both my parents were deaf.

I was my family's ears.

2

Hidden Stars

HERTA: MY NAME IS Herta Myers. I'm Renee's younger sister. I was born two years after her, in 1935. When I was a little girl, I was the only deaf child in our town. In our family there were several deaf people like me, going back a few generations, including both our parents: our mother, Henrietta, and our father, Julius. We communicated using sign language.

RENEE: We grew up in Bratislava, the capital of what was then called Czechoslovakia. Many years after World War II, Czechoslovakia was split into two independent states, the Czech Republic and Slovakia. Back then, Bratislava was a city of 120,000 people, including 15,000 Jews. In 1939, when the Nazis occupied our city, most of our country was renamed the Slovak Republic, which was then controlled by Germany. Many ethnic Germans lived in and around Bratislava.

Jews living in Bratislava's more elegant neighborhoods were ordered to leave their homes and move into what was called the Old Town, which was a ghetto for the poor. That was where my family began living, in an apartment on the fourth floor of an old four-story brick building. In warm weather, my sister and I grew peas by wrapping them in wet cotton balls. We put the balls into little pots of soil on the windowsill and watched over the next few weeks as pea tendrils sprouted and curled up around the iron railings of the window. From our window, we could also peer down in the evening and see our father returning from his office.

Because the Nazis forbade Jewish children from attending school, I did not start my formal education until after the war, when I was almost twelve years old. By then the only subject I didn't have to catch up on was reading, which my father had started teaching me when I was five years old. I remember how much joy I felt when my parents gave me several books for my fifth birthday. That year my mother was often annoyed with me, because I never answered when she called me. My nose was always buried in my books.

HERTA: Our parents were intelligent people, but because they could not hear, they did not attend a typical college. Instead, they went to the Vienna School for the Deaf. After graduating, my father became a master jeweler, and my mother worked as a dressmaker.

RENEE: Once the Nazis occupied Bratislava in 1939, they regularly entered the homes of Jews and forced them to turn over their jewelry and silverware. Because my father was an expert jeweler, the Slovak firm he worked for ordered him to melt down the stolen silver and use it to make chalices and crosses for local churches. I remember him coming home with designs for these objects and looking so sad.

HERTA: At first my parents wanted me to go to the School for the Deaf like they had done, but after the Nazis took over our city, my parents were scared that I would go to school one day and never come back. So we moved about seventy miles west of Bratislava to Brno, where there was a big Jewish community, and for a while we did feel more comfortable there.

My father tried to homeschool me, but I was lazy and had no interest in most subjects. I'd tell him, "Oh, let's do that subject tomorrow—or maybe the day after." Then I would run outside and walk around Brno with my sister, Renee. Because I was deaf, I had to rely on her to be my playmate, and there were times I complained to my mother that I felt lonely. My mother was always willing to give me her time and attention, so despite the loneliness, I considered myself a happy child.

~∽

RENEE: I have one recollection of the German presence at that time, which was when Hitler came through Brno in a car surrounded by Nazi soldiers. All the non-Jews of Brno ran into the streets, cheering and waving Nazi flags, and I remember my father telling me and Herta to stay away from the crowds.

"We are not going to show any support," he said.

I'm sure there was more to it than what my father was saying. He must have known it would be dangerous for us as Jewish children to go outside with so many non-Jews in the streets, cheering Hitler. My father was no doubt afraid that some harm would come to us. As a six-year-old child, I had no idea about politics, although I recall feeling comfortable and uncomfortable at the same time—comfortable because I spoke German like many people around us, but uncomfortable because most of our neighbors hated us because we were Jews.

My parents must have decided things would get worse now that Hitler had visited Brno, and so they announced we would immediately be returning to Bratislava. We had heard what Nazis did to Jews: The Germans arrested them and sent them to "resettlement" camps. In those days, we had not yet heard the name "concentration camps," but whatever they were called, we knew the camps were dangerous for Jews. To avoid the risk of being arrested and sent to a camp, we packed our bags and returned to our apartment in Bratislava.

Back in Bratislava, at first nothing happened to us. German soldiers there just patrolled the streets as usual. Then it got worse. The soldiers began beating up Jews, and local antisemitic Slovaks also abused us and called us "Dirty Jews!" and other nasty things when we passed them in the street.

The abuse got worse once the Nazis forced all Jews to sew a yellow star—the Star of David, a symbol of the Jewish people—on their outer clothing. That was the Nazis' way of singling us out in public. One day Herta and I came home and saw our mother sewing yellow cloth stars on our coats.

"Let's not do this," I signed to her. "If we wear the star, then we can't hide the fact that we are Jews, and it will be worse for us."

"We have no choice," she signed with sadness. "We have to wear the star. It's the law."

Wearing that star was going to make life harder for me and my sister, since we loved to roam freely around the city. We came up with the idea of wearing scarves and draping them around our shoulders so they covered the stars on our coats. That worked for a while, and we continued wandering around Bratislava. Still, we were afraid.

What will happen to us, I wondered, *if they find out we're Jews?*

ABOUT THE AUTHORS

RENA FINDER was born in Krakow, Poland, and survived the Holocaust. Following the war, Rena moved to the United States with her husband, where she raised a family. Rena has dedicated herself to teaching people about "history's darkest hour" and about the need to always speak out against injustice. She has shared her story with schools, colleges, and synagogues over the years, and she is a founding survivor of Facing History and Ourselves.

JOSHUA M. GREENE produces books and films about the Holocaust including *Signs of Survival: A Memoir of the Holocaust* and *Unstoppable: Siggi B. Wilzig's Astonishing Journey from Auschwitz Survivor and Penniless Immigrant to Wall Street Legend.* His documentaries have been broadcast in twenty countries and his books translated into eight languages. He has taught Holocaust history for Fordham and Hofstra Universities.